AR PTS
1.0
AR RL
6.7

DUE

THE LIBRARY OF
nutrition™

Food for Fuel
The Connection Between Food and Physical Activity

Betsy Dru Tecco

rosen central™

The Rosen Publishing Group, Inc., New York

To Sianna and Elise—for the best health & fitness

Published in 2005 by The Rosen Publishing Group, Inc.
29 East 21st Street, New York, NY 10010

First Edition

Library of Congress Cataloging-in-Publication Data

Tecco, Betsy Dru.
Food for fuel: the connection between food and physical activity / by Betsy Dru Tecco.—1st ed.
    p. cm. — (The Library of nutrition)
Includes bibliographical references.
ISBN 1-4042-0303-6 (library binding)
1. Teenagers—Health and hygiene—Juvenile literature. 2. Nutrition—Juvenile literature. 3. Physical fitness—Juvenile literature. 4. Weight loss—Juvenile literature. 5. Obesity—Prevention—Juvenile literature. 6. Exercise—Physiological aspects—Juvenile literature.
I. Title. II. Series.
RA777.T435 2004
613.2'083—dc22

2004014860

Manufactured in the United States of America

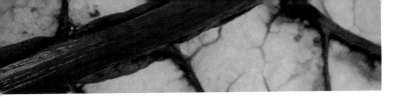

contents

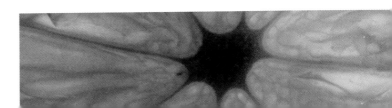

introduction

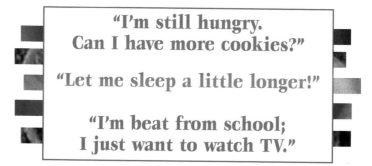

> **"I'm still hungry.**
> **Can I have more cookies?"**
>
> **"Let me sleep a little longer!"**
>
> **"I'm beat from school;**
> **I just want to watch TV."**

If this sounds like you, it may be an indication that your batteries are low. To be more exact, you need energy. Bodies are like electronic gadgets that need power to work. They need to be charged regularly to keep going.

Our bodies don't have built-in batteries. We have to provide them with energy. So, where do we get that energy pack we need for life? We get it from food, sleep, and exercise.

Food gives us energy. The main form of energy used by all our body parts is glucose, which is broken down from carbohydrates, the body's primary source of energy. Eating three balanced meals a day, along with healthy snacking, keeps your blood sugar and energy steady. A balanced diet is one that gives you the right amounts of carbohydrates, fat, protein, vitamins, minerals, and water. These basic nutrients give you the energy to do all the things you do, help your body to break down and use the food you eat,

People who are physically active generally enjoy better health and live longer than those who are not. Playing games such as volleyball regularly with friends is a great way of getting a workout.

regulate temperature, and perform many other functions. Without them, you would have no get-up-and-go!

Sleep helps us to feel rested and energetic. Your body needs rest to grow and repair. You don't get that kind of rest from watching television, sitting at the computer, or playing video games. Sitting around means being sedentary. Sedentary activities make you sluggish, as though someone pushed your "pause" button. After sitting for a long time, you have to move around a bit to get going again. The right kind of rest requires sleep—head on pillow, eyes shut, snoring optional. Middle school kids need about ten hours of sleep each night to be well rested.

Exercise gives us energy. Physical activity revs you up. It brings oxygen to the brain to help you think more clearly. It brings oxygen to the muscles to build your strength and endurance. Aerobic exercise is a natural way of boosting your energy.

Without the right measure of good nutrition, rest, and regular exercise, your body gets out of whack. Like a toy with a weak battery, your systems slow down, affecting how you act, look, and feel.

Emotional Energy

What's your mood like today? Did you know that what you eat and what you do can influence whether you're happy or not? Food and physical activity trigger chemicals in the body called neurotransmitters that send messages back and forth between your brain and your body. These messages control sleep, thoughts, actions, mood, appetite, and more. Skipping meals, eating too much sugar, or drinking too much caffeine can put you in a bad mood. Healthy food can make you happy. For example, foods like oranges and potatoes that are high in vitamin C release serotonin, a neurotransmitter that relaxes and calms you. Exercise releases neurotransmitters called endorphins, which ease pain, reduce stress, and make you feel good.

**FACT!**

About 15 percent of kids in the United States have too much body fat. If you are an overweight kid, you are more likely to be overweight as an adult.

The next time you're feeling sad or nervous, stay away from junk food. It won't solve your problems. However, it can make you gain weight. Instead, go outside and play! Chances are that you will feel better.

Weight Managers

Eating right and exercising regularly help you manage your weight by keeping the proper amount of body fat on your body. Carrying around too much body fat can tire you out. If you weigh 20 percent more than your recommended weight, you're obese. Obesity can lead to many health problems, including heart disease, diabetes, high blood pressure, stroke, and cancer.

Obesity is now the most common risk factor for disease in children and young adults in the United States. The U.S. government is leading a campaign to encourage American children to get in shape by eating well and staying active.

This book provides easy-to-digest facts about how food and physical activity work together to make you fit. It helps you look at your own habits so that you can make changes for better health, better performance, a better body, a better life, a better YOU!

chapter 1

You Control Your Weight

I t's no fun to be the target of a fat joke or chosen last for a team because you're overweight. If you're teased or feel embarrassed about your weight, do you avoid people and sports, escape to the television or computer, or eat food for comfort? Such actions only lead to more weight gain. If that bad cycle isn't broken, it becomes a lifelong habit.

Being too thin can be tough, too. You might be called names like "Beanpole" or "Sticks." Fitting into cool clothes can be hard when you're too thin or too heavy.

The good news is YOU can control your weight. YOU decide what you eat and how much you eat. YOU decide how active you are or whether you spend your free time watching television or shooting hoops.

Think of food as energy you take into your body. Energy is measured in calories. The more calories there are in food, the more energy it contains. A candy bar contains a lot of energy. A head of lettuce contains very little. One candy bar, in fact, supplies the same energy calories as six

Junk food is a prominent feature in the American diet. Many nutrition experts fault this as a leading cause of the alarming rate of obesity in this country, especially among children and young adults.

heads of lettuce, according to Faith Hickman Brynie, author of *101 Questions About Food and Digestion*.

Use Energy Wisely

How much energy you burn depends on a number of factors. These include your activity level, your age, and your body size. Athletes need more energy than couch potatoes because sports are physically demanding. Kids need more energy than adults because they are still growing. Bigger people burn more calories than smaller people because the more a person weighs, the more the body has to work.

Playing soccer and other team sports is a fun way to burn calories. There is also the added benefit of building friendships.

You're always using energy no matter what you're doing. Your body uses energy just to stay alive. Between the ages of eleven and fourteen, boys typically need about 2,500 calories and girls typically need about 2,200 calories daily to meet their energy needs. If you are more active than your peers, you will need extra calories because the more you move, the more energy you need. For example, jumping rope takes more energy than brushing your teeth because your muscles as well as your heart and lungs have to work harder.

Keep a Good Balance

Although the cause of obesity is not completely understood, it basically comes down to this: the amount of calories you eat and the amount you use is out of balance. This is true for everyone.

A neutral energy balance is achieved when you take in as many calories from food as you use for energy. Your body weight remains constant. Unless you need to gain or lose weight, your aim should be to have a neutral energy balance.

A negative energy balance results when you take in fewer calories than you use for energy. Without enough food coming in, the fat stored in your body is used for energy. Your body weight and body fat decrease.

> Calories Consumed = Calories Used = Weight Control
> Calories Consumed < Calories Used = Weight Loss
> Calories Consumed > Calories Used = Weight Gain

Some kids who don't feel good about their appearance overexercise and undereat in an effort to look like a supermodel or a movie star. That's unrealistic. Instead of obsessing over a certain image, focus on having a healthy body.

Do not make it a habit to eat—especially junk food—while watching television. Sedentary practices are a sure way of gaining weight.

Remember, just because you're thin doesn't mean you're fit. If you are thin but inactive, you are probably less fit than someone who is over-weight but stays active. Also, eating too little can lead to health problems such as anemia. Girls can miss their periods. Your bones may not develop completely, which increases your risk of injury and prevents you from reaching your full adult height.

A positive energy balance results when you take in more calories than you use. The excess food is stored as fat in your body. Your body gets bigger, and your weight gets heavier as more and more fat gets tucked away. If you are overweight, you want to avoid more unwanted weight gain.

When it comes to eating, here are some helpful do's and don'ts:

- ○ Do eat slowly.
- ○ Do avoid junk foods.
- ○ Do listen to your body and eat only when you're hungry.
- ○ Don't eat just because you're bored or bummed out.
- ○ Don't skip meals.

Overeating, however, is not the main reason for obesity. Inactivity is the main culprit. We live in a world that makes it too easy to get what we need with very little physical effort. Just think of how often you ride the bus or ride in a car to go places instead of walking or bicycling.

Pick Up the Pace

If you are obese, you need to use more calories than you consume. The best plan tackles both your eating habits and your exercise habits. Cut back on foods with lots of calories and little nutritional value. That means junk food. Most important, use more energy by being physically active throughout the day.

Exercise makes you burn energy much faster than you do when you are resting. For example, twenty minutes of sleeping burns around 10 calories while twenty minutes of running burns around 300.

Exercise keeps your digestive system healthy. A healthy digestive system is able to absorb and deliver nutrients throughout the body efficiently.

FACT!

About 50 percent of American kids and more than 60 percent of adults are not physically active on a regular basis.

Many aerobic exercise machines provide useful information, such as the number of calories burned, about the workout session.

Exercise also preserves and builds muscles. Muscle is healthy lean tissue that helps your body burn calories and use fat. We can't live without muscles. Dieting without exercise leads to the loss of essential muscle.

Making small changes in your physical activity can make a big difference in your calorie-burning potential. If you weigh 100 pounds, you will burn only forty-eight calories watching an hour of television. You can burn that same amount in a quarter of the time by walking a dog. Take the stairs instead of the escalator at the mall. Walking up stairs burns about eighteen calories per minute.

After-School Strategy

What do you do after school? You may be dragging when you come home, but it's your brain that's tired—not your body! The best thing to do after a day in the classroom is play outside for thirty minutes.

CALORIES IN, CALORIES OUT

The chart below shows the caloric value of some popular kid foods and approximately what it would take to burn off those calories.

FOOD	CALORIC VALUE	ACTIVITY TO BURN OFF*
One six-inch carrot	20 calories	5 minutes of skateboarding
A bowl of cereal & skim milk	170 calories	30 minutes of bike riding
One slice of cheese pizza	300 calories	1 hour of soccer
Large order of french fries	540 calories	1 hour of half-court basketball
An eight-ounce soft drink	105 calories	1 hour of washing dishes
One scoop of ice cream	400 calories	2 hours of walking
One cup of low-fat yogurt	61 calories	30 minutes of playing Frisbee

*Figures are based on a 100-lb person

Homework can wait. This will give your brain a break. Plus, your body will get a calorie-burning energy boost.

Before playing, drink a big glass of water with a snack. Not having enough water in your body can cause fatigue, too. Be careful not to eat so much that you blow your appetite for dinner. For a satisfying and nutritious snack, try an apple or a banana, with a spoonful of peanut butter or a slice of cheese.

chapter 2

Food for Fitness

F ood is fun to eat, but what does it really do? Food provides the basic nutrients required for growing, repairing, and maintaining every part of your body. Food and beverages provide the water that every cell of your body needs to function and to keep you cool during exercise. Food also provides the energy needed to fuel the body during athletic training and competition. Without the right amount and mix of food as well as sufficient water, you may find yourself:

- ○ Hungry
- ○ Irritable
- ○ Unable to concentrate
- ○ Losing weight
- ○ Tired
- ○ Missing your period (if you're female)
- ○ Frequently injured or sick
- ○ Not growing properly

Energy Givers

Most of your daily calories—50 to 60 percent—should come from complex carbohydrates such as whole grains found in cereals, bread, rice, and pasta, as well as potatoes, fruits, and vegetables. Growing bodies depend on these powerhouse foods. Your body slowly digests and breaks down complex carbohydrates into glucose. Glucose is taken from the bloodstream to be used as the main source of energy. If it's not needed right away, the glucose hangs out in the muscles and liver as glycogen. Any stored glycogen that isn't used for energy within a day or two goes into long-term storage as fat.

Sugar Highs and Lows

Simple carbohydrates are found in processed foods like candy, cakes, and cookies. They are broken down into glucose quickly so that your body gets a giant jolt of fast energy. Just one candy bar can

Whole-wheat bread as well as various pastas and grains are some sources of carbohydrates, which are the body's main source of energy.

give you a sugar high, but that good feeling only lasts about one hour before your body says, "Enough!" It can't handle too much glucose in the bloodstream at one time, so it sweeps it all into storage. When this

The Food Pyramid

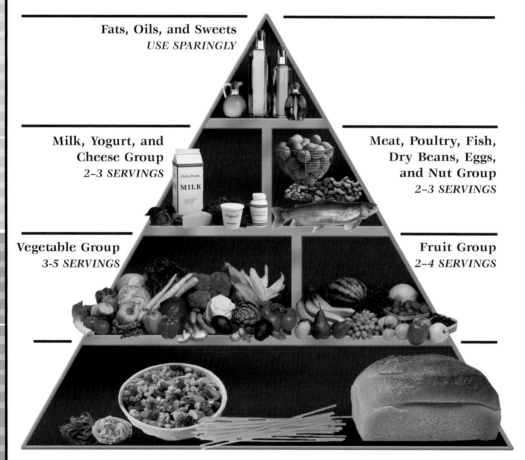

Fats, Oils, and Sweets
USE SPARINGLY

Milk, Yogurt, and
Cheese Group
2–3 SERVINGS

Meat, Poultry, Fish,
Dry Beans, Eggs,
and Nut Group
2–3 SERVINGS

Vegetable Group
3-5 SERVINGS

Fruit Group
2–4 SERVINGS

Bread, Cereal, Rice, and Pasta Group
6-11 SERVINGS

The federal government publishes the food guide pyramid to help us make wise choices about the way we eat.

happens, you have less glucose available for energy than you would have had without the candy. You begin to feel tired, hungry, and cranky. Now your low blood sugar level makes you want to eat again. If you choose another sugary treat, you'll fall into the same trap.

Your blood sugar will be low if you miss a meal, too. So, to keep your energy steady, eat small and frequent meals throughout the day. It also helps with weight control because eating smaller, more frequent meals keeps the rate at which you burn calories steady and higher throughout the day.

Breakfast Rocks!

After sleeping all night, your body is begging for breakfast. It's the most important meal of the day because it kick-starts your body's engine. Start the day with a well-balanced breakfast like a bowl of cereal with milk, a slice of whole-grain toast, and a glass of juice.

Research has found that kids who eat breakfast before school improve their test scores, miss fewer days of school, are happier, and are

Doughnuts are deep-fried breads that are coated with sugar. They are loaded with calories but provide little nutritional value.

This collection of protein-rich foods includes beef, eggs, cheese, and various nuts. In recent years, a number of high-protein–low-carbohydrate diets have become popular in the United States. The benefits and pitfalls of this approach are still being debated.

more energetic. They also have more strength and endurance, concentrate better, and solve problems more easily.

Muscle Makers

Protein has a crucial role to play. Its main purpose is to grow and repair all of our body tissues, including the muscles, tendons, bones, organs, teeth, hair, and skin. Protein is used as an emergency source of energy only when you aren't eating enough food, particularly carbohydrates. Protein-rich food includes all kinds of meat, fish, milk, eggs, peas, beans, and nuts. Between 15 and 20 percent of your calories should come from protein.

Fat's Function

Too much fat is unhealthy, but it isn't all bad. Fat protects our vital organs. It stores and helps our bodies use certain vitamins. It keeps us warm. Also, it makes us feel full so we don't keep eating. Stored fat is used for energy when the body is very active for long periods. Growing bodies need about 25 to 30 percent of caloric intake to come from fat. Some fats are better for us than others. The best are unsaturated fats containing essential fatty acids, which help keep our bodies healthy. Unsaturated fats include plant oils like olive, soybean, canola, corn, sunflower, and peanut oil. Sad to say, the saturated fats in butter, cakes, and ice cream are the bad guys.

Water's Wonder

Water makes up about two-thirds of your body. Take just 15 percent away and you'd probably look like a very tall toothpick. This is a silly way of saying that you can't live without water! Water is important to digestion because it assists in breaking down and absorbing nutrients. It then helps to deliver those nutrients through the bloodstream and to all parts of your body. It helps your muscles to contract. It keeps your body at the right temperature. Water also ends up as urine and sweat, removing waste from your body.

For water to do all that work, it must be constantly replenished. You need to drink about six to eight cups of fluid every day. If you don't get it, your body suffers. You may feel weak and lightheaded. Go more than a few days without water and your body will shut down completely. Juice and milk count toward your fluid needs, as do juicy fruits, vegetables, and soups.

Micronutrients

The word "micro" means "small." Vitamins and minerals are called micronutrients because we need only small quantities of them. Although they don't supply energy, vitamins and minerals are vital because they do keep the body working right.

Consider your bones. Between the ages of nine and fourteen, your bones are growing to their max, although you will continue to build bone mass throughout your early twenties. To reach their full size and become strong, bones need the nourishment of food and the work of exercise. You can't build your bones without calcium. This mineral is found in dairy products such as milk and cheese, leafy green vegetables, and fish such as salmon. You also need vitamin D to help your body absorb calcium. Milk and egg yolks are good sources of vitamin D. Millions of kids are getting too little of this bone-building vitamin, partly because they are chugging soft drinks instead of milk. Another mineral second only to calcium in bone building is phosphorous. It is found in eggs, milk, and meats. Drinking too many soft drinks actually pulls this mineral from your bones.

Healthy bones need exercise, too, because the pull of muscle against bone tells the body to grow bigger and stronger bones. If you get too little exercise, your bones are not as strong as they could be.

Exercise is also crucial for a healthy heart and good circulation, but it isn't enough. You also need two other minerals: iron and potassium. Iron helps bring oxygen to your body. A lack of iron can lead to a loss of strength and endurance; exercise will tire you out faster. To make sure you have enough iron, eat red meat, egg yolks, beans, nuts, green vegetables, and raisins. Potassium helps your heart beat and your muscles move. It is found in bananas, oranges, peanuts, peas, beans, potatoes, yogurt, and meat.

Food and the Playing Field

If you're an athlete, you have the same basic nutritional needs as the kid in your class who spends recess on the computer. You just need more. The longer and harder you exercise, the more calories you need to consume because sports and other physical activities demand a lot of energy.

Milk is an excellent source of calcium, which helps to build strong bones.

What you eat directly affects what you do on game day. When you're pushing your body to perform at its peak level, you need to eat food packed with the nutrients that will make you strong and healthy. You need the nutrients that build, repair, and maintain your body. You need the food that will provide the energy you need to play. That's energy on top of what your body already must have for daily life and growth spurts! So what's the best plan for feeding an active body?

It's especially important to be well fueled before you start exercising. Without the right amount and type of food, your chance of getting sick or

Recipe: FRUIT SMOOTHIE

DRINK FOR ENERGY!

Throw together a super-simple fruit smoothie for fast nutrition.

Ingredients:

Your favorite fruit, such as a banana,
   frozen blueberries, or strawberries

1/2 cup of low-fat milk

1 Tbsp of honey (optional)

5 ice cubes

1/4 cup of low-fat vanilla yogurt

2 tsp of wheat germ (optional)

Put all the ingredients into a blender and blend until smooth.

injured increases. If you participate in after-school sports, eat a good breakfast, a midmorning snack, a hearty lunch at noon, and a small snack at around 2 PM. Good snacks are fruit, yogurt, peanut butter or cheese crackers, granola bars, and low-sugar, high-fiber cereals like Cheerios and Wheat Chex. If you skip that last snack and then have sports practice around 3 to 4 PM, you may feel shaky and light-headed.

Don't overeat, however. A full belly may make you feel so uncomfortable that you don't play well. Besides, food that's still in your stomach and not digested won't help you during a game.

Win with Water

Notice how you sweat while playing a sport? You may even pant like a dog. Well, a lot of water is lost during vigorous exercise. If you don't drink

Tennis star Venus Williams takes a water break during a match in the 2000 French Open tournament in Paris, France. It is essential to drink water during a workout or game to avoid dehydration, which lowers performance.

enough water, you may become dehydrated. Dehydration makes it harder for the body to do its work and interferes with sports performance. It can cause headaches, pain, and fatigue. Experts recommend drinking 16 ounces (or 2 cups) of water approximately an hour before an activity. (One gulp equals about one ounce.) Drink 6 ounces (or 3/4 cup) about every fifteen to twenty minutes during the activity, and 16 ounces (or 2 cups) per pound of weight loss within two hours of the activity. Also, after exercising, eat a snack with protein and carbohydrates to help your muscles recover faster.

chapter 3

Fitting in Physical Activity

The more physically fit you are, the more energy you expend and the more control you have over your weight. During exercise, unfit kids get tired quickly. This limits their ability to burn calories. But if they stick with an exercise program, their fitness level will improve. As they work out harder, longer, and more frequently, they will use up more calories and do more with less fatigue.

Are you physically fit? It depends on more than the food you put in your body. To be physically fit, you need four things:

1: Heart/Lung Strength Your heart is your most important muscle. It beats about 100,000 times a day—up to three times faster during exercise! The blood carries oxygen and nutrients to all parts of your body. All muscles need oxygen to work. The harder your muscles work, the more oxygen they need. The lungs bring in the oxygen from the air you breathe. The oxygen then enters the bloodstream to be taken to the muscles.

Cycling provides a great aerobic workout. It helps to build stamina as well as strengthen calf and thigh muscles.

Stretching is an important part of physical exercise. Fitness experts recommend that we stretch every day, especially in the mornings and after a workout.

By doing aerobic exercise on a regular basis you can speed up the delivery and use of oxygen to produce more energy. "Aerobic" simply means activity in the presence of oxygen. Aerobic exercise strengthens your heart and lungs because it requires more oxygen. This makes your heart and lungs work harder. Over time, they become more efficient at their jobs, which improves your fitness. When you're fit, you can work and play longer before getting tired. You're also less likely to get heart disease and other ailments. Good types of aerobic exercise are fast walking, jogging, bicycling, jumping rope, and swimming.

2: Joint and Muscle Flexibility Elbows, knees, and hips are types of joints. Every joint has an ideal range of motion. If you can easily bend your joints through their entire range of motion, you're flexible. Flexible joints allow you to move like a limber tiger instead of a stiff tin soldier. Short, tight muscles limit flexibility. Unless you've been stretching your muscles regularly, you've already lost some of the flexibility you had as a baby. Stretching exercises help lengthen the muscles, allowing the joints to move fully.

3: Muscle Strength and Endurance The strength of a muscle is the ability to exert force over a short period of time, like carrying a heavy trash can out to the curb. Endurance is the muscle's ability to do something over and over again, like rowing a boat. Both muscle strength and endurance are important. Well-conditioned muscles are less likely to get tired. This means you can do activities longer, better, and with less chance of injury. To train your muscles, you need to work them against some form of resistance. When you do a push-up, for example, your muscles are working against the weight of your body. Your muscles can also work against the weight of objects such as dumbbells or weight machines.

4: Body Composition Our bodies are made up of fat weight and lean body weight. Lean body weight consists of all the tissues of the body other than fat, including the organs, bones, and muscles. To be physically fit, you shouldn't have too much body fat. Young male bodies should be composed of 10 to 15 percent fat. Young female bodies should be composed of 17 to 22 percent fat.

FACT!

U.S. children today are less fit than they were a generation ago, and many are showing early signs of cardiovascular disease.

Doing push-ups is great exercise for beginners. It is a strength exercise that works on the chest, shoulders, arms, abdomen, and lower back.

Exercise and good nutrition are the keys to physical fitness. Exercise makes you feel and look better. It keeps your body at a healthy weight by using energy from the food you eat.

Being active is a choice you make. Any kind of physical movement or activity is worthwhile, even chores like cleaning your room! Did you know you're more likely to be overweight if you eat while watching TV? Instead of plugging in the video games after school, go outside and monkey around. If you make exercise fun, you'll be more motivated to get moving. Pick physical activities that you enjoy and make you feel good about yourself. Get your friends and family to join you. To keep your interest up, mix up the activities. It can be a bore doing the same old thing, and then you won't bother.

How Much Is Enough?

The American College of Sports Medicine recommends at least twenty-five minutes of moderate physical activity three days a week for better health. An hour is even better! Moderate aerobic activities include

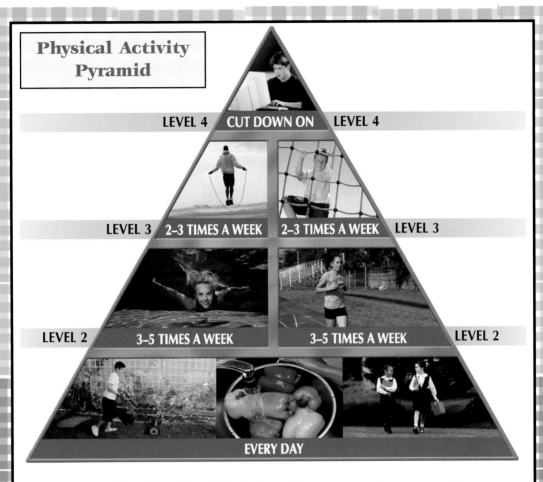

Physical Activity Pyramid

LEVEL 4 — CUT DOWN ON — LEVEL 4

LEVEL 3 — 2–3 TIMES A WEEK — 2–3 TIMES A WEEK — LEVEL 3

LEVEL 2 — 3–5 TIMES A WEEK — 3–5 TIMES A WEEK — LEVEL 2

EVERY DAY

Level 4: Inactivity—Watching TV, playing video or computer games, sitting more than thirty minutes at a time. Limit the time you spend sitting around.

Level 3: Flexibility Exercise, Strength/Muscular Development Exercise—Leisure activities such as dancing, martial arts, skipping rope, push-ups, sit-ups, weight training, and stretching. Do several times per week.

Level 2: Active Aerobics, Sports, and Recreational Activities—Aerobic exercises include swimming, cycling, jogging, brisk walking, playing basketball, etc. Do almost every day, three to five times per week.

Level 1: Lifestyle Activities—Climbing stairs, walking to school, sweeping, washing, and playground play. Do every day.

Try to build physical activities into your daily life. These should include a mixture of play, chores, and formal exercise.

playground games and backyard fun that make you sweaty and your heart beat faster. It includes sports like tennis and basketball. It also includes challenging work like pushing a lawn mower, raking leaves, and shoveling snow.

To improve your total fitness, aerobic exercise should be combined with resistance exercises to increase muscle strength and endurance. Try push-ups, chin-ups, and abdominal curls (curl-ups). If those exercises are too hard, try weight training using light dumbbells, elastic tubing, or exercise balls. A fitness professional can teach you how to weight train safely. Stretching exercises should also be performed to increase flexibility and lower the chance of injury. One good stretch is to sit on the floor with your legs straight in front of you, then reach forward, trying to touch your toes with your fingers. Hold the stretch for about thirty seconds, without bouncing.

To burn off excess fat, choose moderate aerobic exercise that you can do nonstop for at least twenty-five minutes rather than heavy exercise that wears you out fast. During the first twenty minutes or so of exercise, your body is mainly using glycogen for energy. After that, your body relies more on stored fat as energy.

Just Walk More!

Experts say it takes only 10,000 steps a day to become physically fit. During a normal day, you may walk only 5,000 to 6,000 steps. Because most people take about 2,000 steps per mile walked, a person would have to walk only 2 additional miles (3.2 km) to reach the magic number of 10,000. That's about thirty minutes a day of extra walking. To figure out how much you walk in a day, wear a pedometer that measures the number of steps you take. Challenge a friend to see who can walk the most in a day!

chapter 4

Common Myths About Nutrition and Exercise

With all the advice out there about nutrition and physical activity, it should come as no surprise that some of it is just plain wrong. Here are a few of the most popular fitness myths. Don't fall into the trap of using these myths as excuses to continue bad habits like eating poorly and exercising rarely. Understand why they are not true so you can make smarter choices for a healthier life.

Myth: "I'm overweight because I have a slow metabolism." Some people blame a slow metabolism for being obese. Metabolism is a complex process, but basically it refers to the amount of energy (calories) your body burns in a day. Sixty to 70 percent of the calories you use each day goes toward keeping your body operational (organs working, heart pumping, lungs breathing, etc.). Up to 10 percent is used for digesting food and converting it into

Campers participate in a water aerobics exercise at a weight-loss camp in Reeders, Pennsylvania. Camps such as this one have sprung up across the United States in recent years as concerns about obesity grow.

usable energy. The remaining 20 to 30 percent of your metabolism depends on your activity level. That's the part you have control over. Exercise helps boost metabolism. Instead of making excuses for obesity, focus on moving more. By increasing your physical activity, you maintain a healthy, normal weight.

Myth: "Everybody in my family is overweight, so I will be overweight, too." When we see obese parents with obese kids, we are likely to think the problem runs in the family. Obesity is more common in children when their parents are obese. Although it does look like body weight has a strong family link, it doesn't tell the whole story. The basic cause of excess weight and obesity remains the same: you're either eating too much, exercising too little, or both.

Myth: "Exercise will make me hungry, and then I'll eat too much." Exercise may affect how hungry you feel. Studies show that light and moderate exercise tend to decrease your appetite and cause you to eat less at your next meal than normal. You may eat more after a long, vigorous game; however, your weight will likely remain the same because of the extra calories you burned while playing. Even after the game, your body will continue to use energy at a faster rate for several hours. Also, people are more likely to eat too much when they are stressed out or simply bored. Exercise can help you work off frustrations so that you don't pig out.

Myth: "I don't have to exercise because I'm skinny." Some people who are skinny exercise too much. Other people are skinny even though they don't exercise. But that doesn't mean they are physically fit. Some people are underweight but have

Many gyms offer fitness classes to their members. In addition to focusing on proper techniques, the instructors try to make the exercises more fun, which many people find motivating.

excess fat and poorly developed muscles. Exercise is important for more than weight control. Here are just a few more reasons to exercise:

- Improves stamina
- Increases flexibility
- Increases muscle strength and endurance
- Provides stress relief to stay calm and cool
- Boosts immune system to stay healthy
- Enhances appearance
- Improves self-esteem and confidence
- Gives a sense of accomplishment
- Enables one to sleep better
- Feels good
- It's fun!

Myth: "My muscles will turn to fat if I stop exercising." Nothing will change muscle to fat or fat to muscle. That's because muscle and fat are two different kinds of tissue. Muscle fibers look like spaghetti noodles. Fat cells resemble round globs of jelly. Exercise builds up muscle fibers. If you stop exercising, your muscles will weaken and get smaller. Overeating causes fat cells to grow bigger as they store excess fat. The fat cells will shrink if you burn more calories than you eat.

Myth: "Exercise will make me look like the Incredible Hulk." Resistance exercises won't give you bulky muscles. Body builders must work out for hours every day doing specific exercises to develop large muscles. Resistance training is one of the best ways to slim down and improve the body's appearance. Here are more reasons to do strength training:

It is important to learn the proper way of doing exercises. Don't be afraid to seek advice and instruction from your gym teacher, a fitness professional, or someone who knows correct techniques.

- ○ Builds stronger muscles
- ○ Makes bones stronger
- ○ Enhances strength in tendons and ligaments
- ○ Reduces fat
- ○ Creates a higher metabolism
- ○ Achieves greater self-confidence
- ○ Lowers the risk of injury

Myth: "I need to eat a lot of protein to have big muscles." Protein is necessary for muscles to work and for building, keeping, and replacing tissues in the body. However, you need to perform strength-training exercises to grow muscles. You won't get bigger or stronger muscles by eating a ton of protein. A high-protein diet can be dangerous.

Make sure you get most of your nutrients from food. Use vitamin tablets only as supplements to a healthy diet.

It can strain the kidneys, weaken your bones, and lead to weight gain since protein-rich foods are sometimes high in fat. If you eat too much protein and not enough carbohydrates, your body will be forced to use protein for energy. When that happens, protein can't do its job of caring for your muscles, which will make your muscles less powerful. Protein supplements aren't necessary either. To build muscle, exercise regularly and eat a well-balanced diet, choosing lean, healthy protein sources, such as chicken, tuna, eggs, lean beef, and low-fat dairy products.

Myth: "I must be too fat because I weigh too much." If you want to find out how overweight you are, a bathroom scale can't really tell you. Muscle and bone are heavier than fat. That's why it is possible for you to be heavy on the scale and yet lean. Or you might be light on the scale and yet have too much body fat. If you aren't sure about how much body fat you have, ask your family doctor or a qualified fitness or nutrition professional for advice.

Myth: "I have to do abdominal curls to lose the fat around my waist."
When you lose fat, it will occur more in areas of your body with the greatest amount of fat rather than in areas where there is less fat. But you cannot "spot reduce" or target fat loss in any particular body part by performing a certain kind of exercise. You may, however, improve the appearance in that area by increasing muscular development. For instance, abdominal curls can tone and firm the muscles in the area around your tummy.

Three football teammates joke around as they drink water after a game. Water hydrates the body better than any other liquid.

Myth: "Drinking water during exercise will make me sick."
Drinking water will in no way hurt you during exercise. In fact, you should drink a lot of cool water before, during, and after exercise. It is the most important substance you can drink because the body absorbs plain cool water more easily than anything else. Sports drinks are OK if they don't contain too much sugar. Sugar slows absorption. Water helps prevent heat-related illnesses like muscle cramps and heat exhaustion. It also replenishes the fluids lost through sweating.

Conclusion:
Make a Change!

What are your eating and exercise habits? This is an important question to ask yourself every now and then. Bad habits are easy to pick up, but they are hard to break. Sometimes you may not even be aware that you have them. A little self-evaluation is a good first step to achieving proper nutrition and exercise. Take a few minutes to answer the following questions. They will help you identify where you may want to make changes in your life. Change always requires effort, but it's worth the rewards that come from feeling better, looking better, and performing better.

- ○ Do you play active games or sports for at least twenty-five minutes three days each week?
- ○ Do you spend less than two hours per day in front of a television, computer, or video game?
- ○ Do you have at least fifteen minutes of school recess each day?
- ○ Do you have more than thirty minutes of physical education per week?

○ Do you exercise with anyone in your family?

○ Do you eat a wide variety of healthy foods every day?

○ Do you limit foods with high sugar and fat content?

○ Do you eat at least five servings of fruits and vegetables every day?

○ Do you eat a complete breakfast every morning?

○ Do you maintain a healthy body weight?

○ Most of the time, do you eat only when you're hungry?

○ Do you eat a lot of high-fiber foods like whole-grain breads, fresh fruits and vegetables, and beans?

It is important to balance proper nutrition with physical activity. What you eat can influence your game.

○ Do you feel good about your eating and exercise habits?

If you answered "No" to any of those questions, you may want to think about making a change. Believe in yourself. You can do it! You can become stronger and healthier if you try. Think about what you eat and what you do. Each day, choose good foods and find ways to be active. Your wise choices will bring you a richer life!

Glossary

aerobic Any physical activity that requires breathing in oxygen for the working of muscles and lasts for twenty minutes or more to condition the heart and lungs.

carbohydrates One of the essential nutrients that we get from food.

cardiovascular Having to do with the heart and blood vessels.

endurance Your body's ability to withstand hardship or stress.

energy The power to work or act.

glucose A sugar that is the main fuel for body cells, broken down from carbohydrates.

glycogen A starch that is stored in the muscles and liver, which can be converted into glucose for energy.

minerals Chemicals the body needs as nutrients.

nutrient A substance found in foods and drinks that the body needs to be able to grow, heal, and perform daily functions.

protein One of the essential nutrients that we get from food.

tissue The substance that forms the parts of living things, such as your organs.

vitamins Chemicals the body needs as nutrients.

For More Information

National Center for Nutrition and Dietetics
American Dietetic Association
216 West Jackson Boulevard
Chicago, IL 60606-6995
(800) 366-1655
Web site: http://www.eatright.org/Public

President's Council on Physical Fitness and Sports
701 Pennsylvania Avenue NW, Suite 205
Washington, DC 20004
(301) 272-3421
Web site: http://www.fitness.gov

Web Sites
Due to the changing nature of Internet links, the Rosen
Publishing Group, Inc., has developed an online list of
Web sites related to the subject of this book. This site is
updated regularly. Please use this link to access the list:

http://www.rosenlinks.com/linu/fofu

For Further Reading

Bean, Anita. *Kids' Food for Fitness: The ABCs of Healthy Eating and Sports Nutrition for Active Kids.* Alameda, CA: Hunter House, 2003.

Brynie, Faith Hickman. *101 Questions About Food and Digestion.* Brookfield, CT: Twenty-First Century Books, 2002.

Gavin, Mary, Neil Izenberg, and Steven Dowshen. *Fit Kids.* New York: DK Publishing, 2004.

Haduch, Bill. *Food Rules!: The Stuff You Munch, Its Crunch, Its Punch, and Why You Sometimes Lose Your Lunch.* New York: Dutton Children's Books, 2001.

Kane, William M. *Health Matters! Volume 4: Physical Activity, Weight, and Eating Disorders.* Danbury, CT: Grolier Publishing, 2002.

Litt, Ann. *Fuel for Young Athletes.* Champaign, IL: Human Kinetics, 2004.

Bibliography

Benardot, Dan, and Walter R. Thompson. "Energy from Food for Physical Activity: Enough and on Time." *ACSM's Health & Fitness Journal*, July/August 1999, pp. 14–18.

Dickey, Thomas, ed. *Fitness, Health, and Nutrition: Setting Your Weight*. Alexandria, VA: Time-Life Books, 1987.

Dintiman, George B., et. al. *Discovering Lifetime Fitness: Concepts of Exercise and Weight Control*. St. Paul, MN: West Publishing Company, 1984.

Fisher, Enid. *Good Health Guides: Food and Health*. Milwaukee, WI: Gareth Stevens Publishing, 1998.

Funderburg, Lise. "The 10 Burning Questions About Metabolism." *OPRAH Magazine*, September 2003, pp. 173–174.

Henner, Marilu, and Lorin Henner. *Healthy Kids: Help Them Eat Smart and Stay Active—For Life!* New York: HarperCollins, 2001.

Hockey, Robert V. *Physical Fitness: The Pathway to Healthful Living*. St. Louis, MO: Mosby-Year Book, Inc., 1996.

Kalish, Susan. *Your Child's Fitness: Practical Advice for Parents*. Champaign, IL: Human Kinetics, 1996.

Manore, Melinda M. "Fueling Exercise." *ACSM's Health & Fitness Journal*, May/June 2000, pp. 34–35.

McGraw, Jay. *Ultimate Weight Solution for Teens: The 7 Keys to Weight Loss Freedom*. New York: Free Press, 2003.

McInnis, Kyle J. "Exercise for Obese Clients." *ACSM's Health & Fitness Journal*, January/February 2000, pp. 25–31.

Mee, Charles L., Jr., , ed. *Fitness, Health, and Nutrition: Building Endurance*. Alexandria, VA: Time-Life Books, 1987.

O'Shea, Michael. "At What Age Can Children Start to Weight Train?" *Parade Magazine*, August 24, 2003, p. 19.

O'Shea, Michael. "Parade's Guide to Better Fitness." *Parade Magazine*, September 21, 2003, p. 12.

Parker, Steve. *Professor Protein's Fitness, Health, Hygiene, and Relaxation Tonic*. Brookfield, CT: Copper Beech Books, 1996.

Powell, Jillian. *Health Matters: Exercise and Your Health*. Austin, TX: Raintree Steck-Vaugn, 1998.

Schwarzenegger, Arnold, and Charles Gaines. *Arnold's Fitness for Kids Ages 11–14: A Guide to Health, Exercise, and Nutrition*. New York: Doubleday, 1993.

Sharkey, Brian J., Ph.D. *Fitness and Health*. 4th Ed. Champaign, IL: Human Kinetics, 1997.

Sothern, Melinda S., T. Kristian von Almen, and Heidi Schumacher. *Trim Kids: The Proven 12-Week Plan that Has Helped Thousands of Children Achieve a Healthier Weight*. New York: HarperCollins Publishers, 2001.

Spence, Annette. *Encyclopedia of Good Health: Nutrition*. New York: Facts on File Publications, 1988.

Tanner, Lindsey. "Teens' Vitamin D Deficiency Brings Worry." Associated Press, 2003.

Uhlman, Marian. "Fitness Is Gaining Weight." *Philadelphia Inquirer*, September 1, 2003.

Index

About the Author

Betsy Dru Tecco has a B.A. in English and writing from Pennsylvania State University. She has written extensively about health and fitness for many publications. This is her tenth book.

Photo Credits

Cover (background images), back cover images, title page (background images), pp. 3, 4, 8, 17, 27, 33, 40 © David Wasserman/Artville; cover image, title image © Phillip and Karen Smith/SuperStock; pp. 5, 10 © Ed Bock/Corbis; pp. 9 © Tim Boyle/Getty Images; p. 12 © Jeff Albertson/Corbis; p. 14 © Photodisc Green/Getty Images; pp. 15, 24, 35 © Royalty-Free/Corbis; p. 17 © Custom Medical Stock Photo; p. 18 © Photodisc/2004 Punchstock except image of fish © Image Club; p. 19 © Jean-Marc Charles/Corbis Sygma; p. 20 © Nathan Benn/Corbis; pp. 23, 41 © Image Bank/Getty Images; p. 25 © Duomo/Corbis; p. 27 © Stone/Getty Images; pp. 28, 37 © Photodisc/2004 Punchstock; p. 30 © Nancy Ney/Corbis; p. 31: top © 2004 Comstock Images, row two (left) © Photodisc Green/2004 Punchstock, row two (right) © Royalty-Free/Corbis, row three (left) © Royalty-Free/Corbis, row three (right) © Maura Burochow, bottom (left) © Royalty-Free/Corbis, bottom (middle) © Royalty-Free/Getty Images, bottom (right) © 2004 Comstock Images; p. 34 © William Thomas Cain/Getty Images; p. 38 © James Leynse/Corbis; p. 39 © Thinkstock/Getty Images.

Designer: Geri Fletcher; **Editor:** Wayne Anderson